IT'S TIME TO EAT VEGETABLE SALAD

It's Time to Eat VEGETABLE SALAD

Walter the Educator

Silent King Books
A WhichHead Entertainment Imprint

Copyright © 2024 by Walter the Educator

All rights reserved. No part of this book may be reproduced in any manner whatsoever without written per- mission except in the case of brief quotations embodied in critical articles and reviews.

First Printing, 2024

Disclaimer

This book is a literary work; the story is not about specific persons, locations, situations, and/or circumstances unless mentioned in a historical context. Any resemblance to real persons, locations, situations, and/or circumstances is coincidental. This book is for entertainment and informational purposes only. The author and publisher offer this information without warranties expressed or implied. No matter the grounds, neither the author nor the publisher will be accountable for any losses, injuries, or other damages caused by the reader's use of this book. The use of this book acknowledges an understanding and acceptance of this disclaimer.

It's Time to Eat VEGETABLE SALAD is a collectible early learning book by Walter the Educator suitable for all ages belonging to Walter the Educator's Time to Eat Book Series. Collect more books at WaltertheEducator.com

USE THE EXTRA SPACE TO TAKE NOTES AND DOCUMENT YOUR MEMORIES

VEGETABLE SALAD

It's time to eat, let's gather near,

It's Time to Eat

Vegetable Salad

A veggie salad full of cheer!

Crunchy, colorful, fresh, and bright,

It's time to take a healthy bite!

Lettuce leaves so crisp and green,

The freshest treat you've ever seen.

Tomatoes red, like tiny suns,

They make the salad so much fun!

Cucumbers cool with stripes so light,

Carrots orange, so crisp and bright.

Bell peppers yellow, red, and green,

A rainbow snack that's fit for a queen!

Broccoli trees stand nice and tall,

Cauliflower clouds, we'll eat them all.

Spinach leaves with a leafy swirl,

Veggies make our tummies twirl!

It's Time to Eat Vegetable Salad

Add some corn, sweet and gold,

Peas so round and fun to hold.

Radish slices, pink and white,

Every veggie brings delight!

Drizzle on dressing, creamy or clear,

Mix it up, the fun is here!

A little crunch, a tasty chew,

Veggie salad is good for you!

Eating greens makes us so strong,

They help us grow our whole life long.

Healthy foods give us the power,

To run and jump and bloom like flowers!

Let's share a bowl, and pass it 'round,

The joy of veggies can be found.

Together we smile and happily say,

It's Time to Eat

Vegetable Salad

"Veggie salad brightens our day!"

Morning, lunch, or dinner too,

Veggie salad is fresh and new.

It's nature's gift, so full of cheer,

Let's eat it up, our feast is here!

One last bite, then we all shout,

"Thank you, veggies, there's no doubt!"

You're good for us, so fresh and true,

It's Time to Eat

Vegetable Salad

Veggie salad is the best to do!

ABOUT THE CREATOR

Walter the Educator is one of the pseudonyms for Walter Anderson. Formally educated in Chemistry, Business, and Education, he is an educator, an author, a diverse entrepreneur, and he is the son of a disabled war veteran. "Walter the Educator" shares his time between educating and creating. He holds interests and owns several creative projects that entertain, enlighten, enhance, and educate, hoping to inspire and motivate you. Follow, find new works, and stay up to date with Walter the Educator™ at WaltertheEducator.com

www.ingramcontent.com/pod-product-compliance
Lightning Source LLC
LaVergne TN
LVHW052016060526
838201LV00059B/4052